Parade to the Guillotine

Phia Clark

BookLeaf Publishing

Presentation by *BookLeaf Publishing*

Web: www.bookleafpub.com

E-mail: info@bookleafpub.com

ISBN: 9789357443173

First edition 2023

To my younger self, I'm happy you got to grow up.

To my future self, keep growing.

ACKNOWLEDGEMENT

To everyone who walked with me on the edge, and then walked me back.

PREFACE

The title of this book came to me while sitting in the college cafeteria, avoiding homework, but it still stuck with me even as I tried to think of "better" names. Quite honestly, this one fits the book well.

Inspired by the 1790s Reign of Terror, the title is a play on how Marie Antoinette was carted down streets and publicly humiliated before her execution in 1793. Marie lived an extravagant life and was widely disliked by her people, but her tragic end was one of the most famous guillotine executions known.

Something about her story and end spoke to me.

This book is not a collection of light-hearted poems or fun rhyming verses. This is the darkest parts of my heart and mind.

While most can't see in the dark, some eyes have simply had to adjust.

Guilt

The feeling will wane
Eventually
It will fade to the back of your mind
Settling like dust
Only to be drawn up when a memory uncovers it
Presumably tugged harshly to the forefront of
your consciousness
Like a sheet from a hidden form
This will ebb, and it will spike, but the thing I've
come to realize
About guilt
Is that it never truly goes away

Love?

What's the point?
One sided
One broken
Moved on like hurricane
Moving fast and leaving carnage
Why am I left clinging to the rags of memories
You've thrown out of mind?
I hate that I let you infest my mind
And tunnel into my heart
But I have no choice
Keeping my grotesque smile
I ignore the tremble and quiver of my cold lips
What's the point
Of love?

Mania

Mania keeps me warm in the cold
Grinning, mad and broad
I dance to a melody no one can hear
High and uncaring
Drunk on the feeling of bubbling laughs in my
chest
I see
But I don't
Every breath is like inhaling a drug so potent it
can make me forget
Forget I care
Forget I cry
Forget that I desperately want to be far, far away
Maina reminds me of why I want to live
But when
In a flash of violet light
It's gone
So does the reminder

Candy Cell

If I could show you
The cell that holds me captive
I would reach into my skull
Moving past the barrier of domed white bone
Into the hollowed-out cradle of my captor
With cold, dead fingers
I would grip the wet, fleshy matter
And rip my tormentor from my body
Leaving me dead
Quiet
And at peace

Live Like a King

Why must I
Swallow down scientifically manufactured
happiness
To feel it?
Is this feeling of anger all I have?
Is this hate and aggression at my core?
Only tampered down by pills
The ones that keep me lulled into a sense of
sanity
Fat and happy like negligent kings
I hope that this kingdom burns
And takes me with it

Sleepless

Whether it's the ever constant
Rapidly running
Stream of the thought
Or simply
The plague of a brightly colored enemy of sleep
That lightens the room
And makes my eyes shine and strain
An ache settles in the dark
The thought that
In The quiet
Sleeplessness of night
I'm worse than alone
I'm alone with myself

Mirror Image

My inner self
Rarely smiles at the mirror
Nowadays
Mostly because the reflection
Is so busy faking one
It no longer needs to

Ring Around

Tears pool
Collecting the corners
Of misty eyes
The look of exhaustion is so pretty
Of self-hate
Of a bone-deep loathing
It's so beautifully unhinged
Sunken eyes and tinted smile
The sickening smell of flowers turned to mist
Disguises a scent of death akin to posies
Much slower
More torturous
A cruel
Drawn out death
Though timeless in tact
A never-ending war strategy
To simply destroy
From within

A New Vice

Distraction
Release
The throw of mindless shapes
Helps ease the pain
But being used
Quickly becomes painful
No other look
Simply one
Simply a piece of meat
Cold and numb
Fake sounds pour from my lips
Similar to the tears that pour down my face
Leaving trials of salt and sorrow
Loneliness keeps me crying
The bed so cold suddenly
The bone deep chill
Tunnels from crawling skin to my very marrow
Feeling dirty
I scrub myself raw
Red and sore
But I can't scrub away the memories of so many
hands

Pining

Plagued by your smile
Consistently reminded of your lack of love
Things make me smile as I think of you
But then falls to a bitter and sad expression
These are the times when I wish I could drown
myself in a bottle
Or fly higher than a kite
I beg the pain to go away
For my heart and head to simply stitch the hole
you ripped into them
You smile
Your eyes
Your laugh
Why can't I stop picturing you
A shy smile aimed at me makes my heart stutter
But when I wake I realize it's still shattered

The Shore

Anger roars in my chest of late
Like waves crash along a jagged shore
Perhaps because I've neglected
My self-severed doses of sanity
Or maybe I've just overwhelmed myself
By constantly holding my breath against the
hateful thoughts
They seep out of my lungs like a toxic gas
I feel them expand
Holding the poisonous words in a too-tight chest
Ribs bloated with the strain of containing such
loathing
Though the unfortunate thing is
This poison can only do two things
Hurt those who breathe it
Or kill those who hold it

The Dahlia

This ache is something I'd almost forgotten
I had grown so much since this blight had
withered me
The sickness made me weak and dying
I had pushed my roots to grow stronger
And my flowers to bloom
But now their petals fall to the ashen ground
And the roots that had found purchase in the
pain
Break and shrivel to uselessness
This fight has grown weary
And maybe if I can put it to rest
New flowers can bloom over my grave

Holding Back

There's a pause
An expanse of air
Sharp
Like the jagged outline of Mountains
Their peaks taking a bite out of a golden horizon
A gaping maw of nature's creation
The pause is tainted
Like women
When he strips the bloodied sheets from her bed
It cuts
Like the blade
That kisses the skin of soft flesh of a pale
forearm
This pause
This intake of breath
The ropes that snap and fray
Holding back the venom you wish to spew
The woven strands wound together
By tested patience
And the very breath that I hold
The words choked and swallowed down
Like a dismal meal
A jaw that grinds And locks
Against the onslaught of
Angry Hateful Whispers

The ones that trick the mind
Into believing tails
Spun fictitiously by strung-up emotions
This pause
Is the last resort
The final straw
Before a door closes
And lock behind it

My Breaking

Hit in the chest
Knocked down
And held there
Caught in a ruthless undertow
The push and pull
Leaving no room for air
The cruel whipping beat of my heart
Lashing against my rib cage
I swear you can hear it
The deafening crack
Of my breaking

Rat

Tears
Unwanted and unwilling
Slip down ruddy cheeks
Blind to consent
You are not welcome here
Why did my lungs stall?
Why do my hands tremble?
Shivering like a fearful rodent
Cornered
Pathetic
Hopeless
Weak
And
Destined to die

Addiction

Held in your disgustingly comforting grip
Locked in your plush cage
Lounging in a prison of my own making
Basking in a demise that belongs solely to me
How does one break a hold
The of something they can't let go of
Finger curled around it
Gripping like a child clinging
To the boned finger of those who hold it
Like a prized possession
It makes you feel safe
Warm and whole like no other
Only to leave you like the sun
Disappearing at dusk
Leaving you shivering in the night

Superficial Scars

Pathetic slits drawn in blood
Rake down my arms
Crossing each other's paths
Like weary strangers
But they won't stay long
Quick to scab and heal
Quick to disappear
And remind me of how weak I am
Sometimes when the moon is pale
And dawn far off
This staggering pain
Feels like a phantoms caress
Not real
But there nonetheless
There is nothing to show
I feel as though there is nothing
No proof of my struggles
Only the tales I tell
Why does it feel like I'm lying
To others
To myself
To my body
For there are no scars

Exasperated (Done)

Life is not fair
So how does one choose
When to judge
When to say that
Life's unfairness
Is exactly what makes it fair?
When does empathy
Warp into pity
Then
Frustration
Then
Resentment
And finally
Abandonment
When do we get to decide
That life's unfairness
Is just
"Too much"

The Golden Rule

Why is the idea
Something simple
And attune to one's own judgment
So extraordinarily difficult
To comprehend
A ripple
On the glass-like water
Of ignorance
The sunshine so bright
The grass so green
When reaped
On the backs of those who you
Believe are not worthy
Ignorant
Audacious
Why must the toy be ripped
From your greedy
Gripping
Fingers
For you to learn how to

Mother Nature's Hour Glass

It's almost soothing
The feeling of time slipping
Through your loose
Numb
Fingers
The grains of sand
Make soft hushing sounds
As they rush to prove your mortality
Some wish to turn back the clock
To erase the past
And relive their decisions
But others
They understand
That time is a serpentine form
Slithering through the universe
Writhing amongst the human disease
An infestation
A cruel
Unforgiving
Selfish
Race
You see
Some find time terrifying
I see it
As a means to an end

Parade to the Guillotine

Quiet and still
Watching the world through
The bars of my mind
I'd like to think that
Somewhere deep inside myself
Lies the answer to all the questions
That bombarded the shallow depths
Of my forethoughts
Stones rattle my cage
As it rumbles down the streets
Of my subconscious
Grinding the bones of my closeted skeletons
That have fallen into its path
To a dust
That whips my face as I sit
The ride is long
Painful
A cruel display
Of my weakness
Of my cursed humanity
I was selfish
I was stupid
And now
I am taking my last shuddering breaths
In confinement

It will be over soon
This parade
This wicked show
Played for the amusement of the sick hearted
Sick minded
Soon the blade will fall
And all will be silenced
The jeers
Shouts
And Curses
All will be well
Once my head is rolling